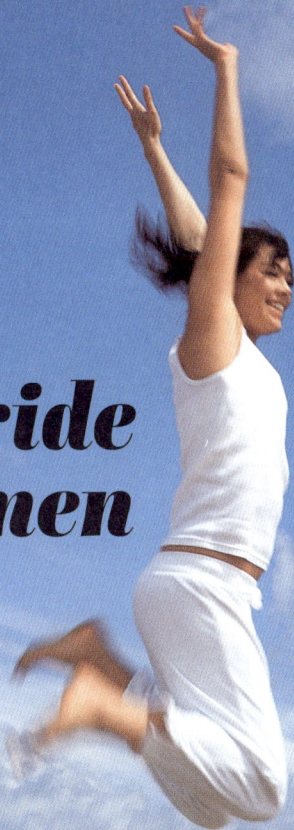

The Stride of Women

The Stride of Women

Mantras and quotes to empower and inspire your walk through life

CICO BOOKS

Published in 2025 by CICO Books
An imprint of Ryland Peters & Small Ltd
20–21 Jockey's Fields
London WC1R 4BW
and
1452 Davis Bugg Road
Warrenton, NC 27589

www.rylandpeters.com
Email: euregulations@rylandpeters.com

10 9 8 7 6 5 4 3 2 1

A CIP record for this book is available from the British Library.
US Library of Congress CIP data has been applied for.

ISBN: 978-1-80065-430-3

Printed in China

Commissioning editor: Kristine Pidkameny
Senior designer: Emily Breen
Art director: Sally Powell
Creative director: Leslie Harrington
Production manager: Gordana Simakovic
Publishing manager: Carmel Edmonds

The authorised representative in the EEA is
Authorised Rep Compliance Ltd.,
Ground Floor. 71 Lower Baggot Street,
Dublin, D01 P593, Ireland
www.arccompliance.com

MIX
Paper | Supporting
responsible forestry
FSC® C106563

INTRODUCTION

"What you want to ignite in others must first burn inside yourself."

Charlotte Brontë

Be empowered to find your path in life, inspired by the words of the incredible women who walked before you and shaped history. From novelists and explorers to early women's rights advocates and social reformers, discover the sage words of both well-known and less familiar female trailblazers—including novelist Mary Wollstonecraft Shelley, aviator Bessie Coleman, physician Sarah Parker Remond, entrepreneur Madame C. J. Walker, and many more.

Within these pages of stirring words and amazing images, you'll find wisdom, motivation, comfort, and joy. Experience them in your solitary moments of personal reflection or share them with others as you connect in social settings, perhaps even while out walking. Maybe choose a mantra or quotation that resonates with you to add to your journal or send to others for inspiration. Feel the dynamic determination of these fascinating women and be encouraged to further explore the rich stories of their lives.

Step into your power and join the ranks of the many remarkable women whose achievements have influenced and contributed to positive change in the world.

WHERE DO WE BEGIN?
BEGIN WITH THE HEART.

I'm stepping out

IT IS GREATER THAN THE STARS—THAT MOVING PROCESSION
OF HUMAN ENERGY; GREATER THAN THE PALPITATING EARTH
AND THE THINGS GROWING THEREON.

Kate Chopin (1850–1904)

American author Kate Chopin was considered to be
a forerunner to feminist writing in the 20th century.

ALL THAT I SAY IS,
EXAMINE, INQUIRE. LOOK INTO
THE NATURE OF THINGS. SEARCH OUT
THE GROUNDS OF YOUR OPINIONS, THE
FOR AND AGAINST. KNOW WHY YOU BELIEVE,
UNDERSTAND WHAT YOU BELIEVE, AND
POSSESS A REASON FOR THE FAITH
THAT IS IN YOU.

Frances Wright (1795–1852)

Frances Wright was a Scottish-born lecturer,
abolitionist, early women's rights advocate,
and social reformer.

I like adventures, and
I'm going to find some.

Louisa May Alcott (1832–1888)

Louisa May Alcott was an American
novelist best known for *Little Women*, as
well as an abolitionist and early feminist.

**One step at a time
is all it takes
to get you there.**

Emily Dickinson (1830–1886)

Considered a leading 19th-century American poet, Emily Dickinson was known for her unique voice and groundbreaking use of language and form.

Truth is the only safe ground to stand on.

Elizabeth Cady Stanton (1815–1902)

American writer, activist, and abolitionist Elizabeth
Cady Stanton was a leader in the women's rights
movement who drafted the first organized demand
for women's suffrage in the United States.

Trust in the path less traveled

My soul is awakened, my spirit
is soaring and carried aloft
on the wings of the breeze.

Anne Brontë (1820–1849)

Anne Brontë was an English poet, novelist, and
the youngest member of the literary Brontë family.

I GOT MY START
BY GIVING MYSELF
A START.

*Madame C. J. Walker
(1867– 1919)*

American entrepreneur, social
activist, and philanthropist
Madame C. J. Walker also created
specialized beauty and hair products
for African-American women.

Oh, never mind the fashion. When one has a style of one's own, it is always twenty times better.

Margaret Oliphant (1828–1897)

Margaret Oliphant was a prolific Scottish novelist and historical writer who was in many ways a trailblazer and a model for later Scotswomen who hoped to make their mark as writers.

STAND TALL AND WALK FOR ALL WOMEN

BEWARE;
FOR I AM FEARLESS, AND
THEREFORE POWERFUL.

Mary Wollstonecraft Shelley
(1797–1851)

An English novelist best known as the author
of *Frankenstein*, Mary Wollstonecraft Shelley
was also the daughter of feminist
philosopher, educator, and writer
Mary Wollstonecraft.

The world is wide, and I will not waste my life in friction when it could be turned into momentum.

Frances Willard (1839–1898)

Frances Willard was an American educator, temperance reformer, and women's suffragist.

The door that nobody else will go in at seems always to swing open widely for me.

Clara Barton (1821–1912)

Clara Barton was an American nurse who founded the American Red Cross.

Be true to yourself and trust in your abilities, for you are capable of greatness beyond measure.

Hatshepsut (c. 1507–1458 BC)

Considered one of Egypt's greatest pharaohs and one of the most prolific builders in Ancient Egypt, Hatshepsut brought great wealth and artistry to her land.

**Never give up,
for that is just the place
and time that the tide
will turn.**

Harriet Beecher Stowe (1811–1896)

An American abolitionist and author of the
best-selling novel *Uncle Tom's Cabin*, Harriet
Beecher Stowe wrote about the harsh conditions
experienced by enslaved African Americans.

You have an appointment with life...

go the distance

One of the eternal truths is that
happiness is created and developed
in peace, and one of the eternal
rights is the individual's right to live.

Bertha von Suttner (1843–1914)

The first woman to be awarded the Nobel Peace
Prize, Bertha von Suttner was an Austro-Bohemian
noblewoman, pacifist, novelist, and author of one of
the 19th century's most influential books,
Lay Down Your Arms.

THE VALUE OF
LIFE DOES NOT DEPEND
UPON THE PLACE WE OCCUPY.
IT DEPENDS UPON THE WAY WE
OCCUPY THAT PLACE.

Thérèse of Lisieux (1873–1897)

Thérèse of Lisieux was a French Carmelite nun,
popularly known in English as "Little Flower,"
who was influential because of her simple
and practical approach to spiritual life.

I will walk where my own nature would be leading.

Emily Brontë (1818–1848)

Emily Brontë was an English novelist and poet, best known for *Wuthering Heights*, her only novel, which is now considered a classic of English literature.

It is only through shadows that one comes to know the light.

St. Catherine of Siena
(1347–1380)

Italian mystic and pious laywoman St. Catherine of Siena engaged in papal and Italian politics through extensive letter-writing and advocacy.

I DID NOT RUN AWAY, I WALKED AWAY BY DAYLIGHT...

Sojourner Truth (c. 1797–1883)

American abolitionist and activist Sojourner Truth fought for African-American civil rights and women's rights.

There is a transcendent
power in example.

Anne Sophie Swetchine (1782–1857)

Anne Sophie Swetchine was a Russian mystic
and social leader famous for her salon in Paris.

THE ARTIST MUST POSSESS THE COURAGEOUS SOUL THAT DARES AND DEFIES.

Kate Chopin (1850–1904)

American author Kate Chopin was
considered to be a forerunner to feminist
writing in the 20th century.

Our first journey is to find that special place for us.

Florence Nightingale
(1820–1910)

The founder of modern nursing, Florence Nightingale was an English social reformer and statistician.

HANG IN THERE.
IT IS ASTONISHING HOW
SHORT A TIME IT CAN TAKE
FOR VERY WONDERFUL THINGS
TO HAPPEN.

Frances Hodgson Burnett (1849–1924)

Frances Hodgson Burnett was a British-American novelist and playwright best known for novels *Little Lord Fauntleroy*, *A Little Princess*, and *The Secret Garden*.

Dare to declare who you are. It is not far from the shores of silence to the boundaries of speech. The path is not long, but the way is deep. You must not only walk there, you must be prepared to leap.

Hildegard of Bingen (c. 1098–1179)

Hildegard of Bingen was a German abbess, visionary mystic, writer, composer, philosopher, and medical practitioner during the High Middle Ages.

There is a stubbornness about me that never can bear to be frightened at the will of others. My courage always rises at every attempt to intimidate me.

Jane Austen (1775–1817)

An English novelist with a lasting legacy of six major published works, including *Pride and Prejudice*, Jane Austen is notable for her wit, social observation, and insights into the lives of early 19th-century women.

I move with dignity, respect.

and inner strength

Courage calls to courage everywhere,
and its voice cannot be denied.

Millicent Garrett Fawcett (1847–1929)

Millicent Garrett Fawcett was an English political
activist and writer who campaigned for women's
suffrage by legal change. She led Britain's largest
women's rights association from 1897 to 1919.

Live life
when you have it.
Life is a splendid
gift—there is nothing
small about it.

Florence Nightingale
(1820–1910)

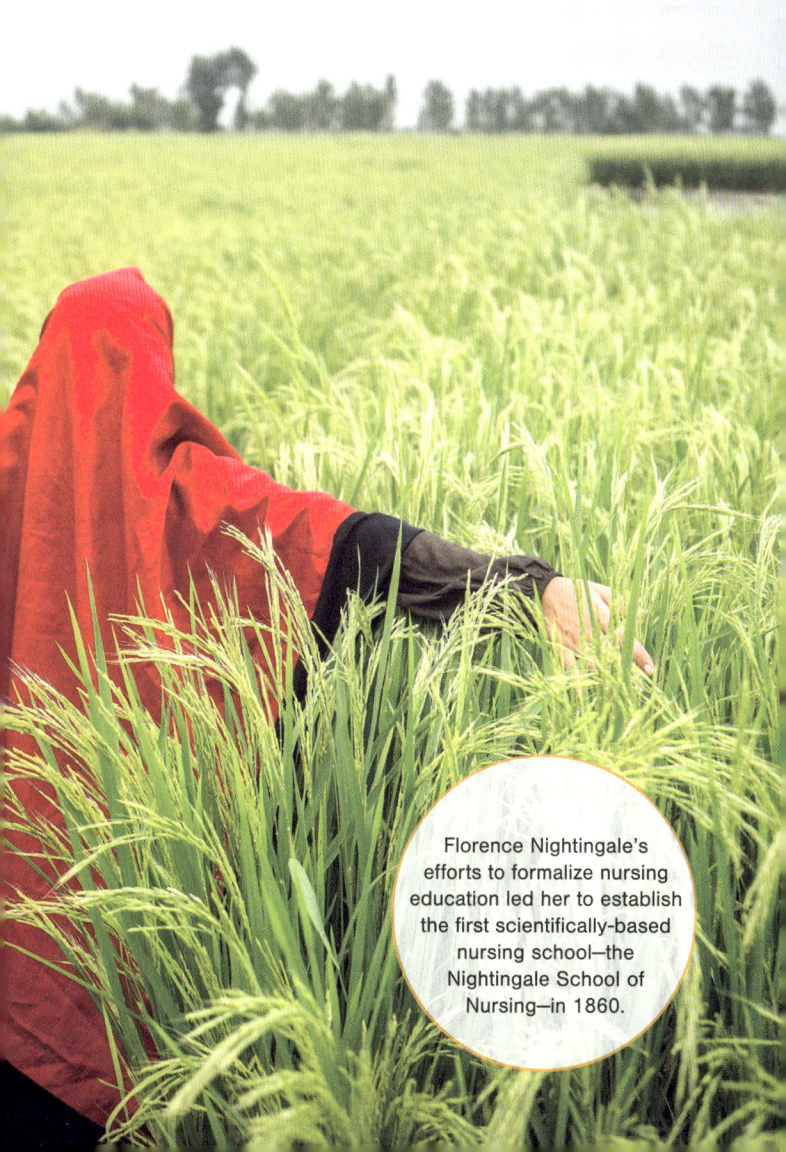

Florence Nightingale's efforts to formalize nursing education led her to establish the first scientifically-based nursing school—the Nightingale School of Nursing—in 1860.

Tell them that as soon as I can walk, I'm going to fly!

Bessie Coleman (1892–1926)

Bessie Coleman was a pilot, advocate, aviator,
and first African-American woman and first
Native American to hold a pilot license.

I will not be triumphed over.

Cleopatra (70/69–30 BC)

An Egyptian queen of Macedonian descent, Cleopatra was the last ruler of the Ptolemaic dynasty in Egypt who actively influenced Roman politics at a crucial period.

We reform others unconsciously
when we walk uprightly.

Anne Sophie Swetchine (1782–1857)

Anne Sophie Swetchine was notable for her
relentless quest for knowledge, her profound faith,
and her unyielding commitment to helping others.

Growth is a spiral process, doubling back
on itself, reassessing and regrouping.

Julia Margaret Cameron (1815–1879)

British photographer Julia Margaret Cameron
was considered one of the most important
portraitists of the 19th century.

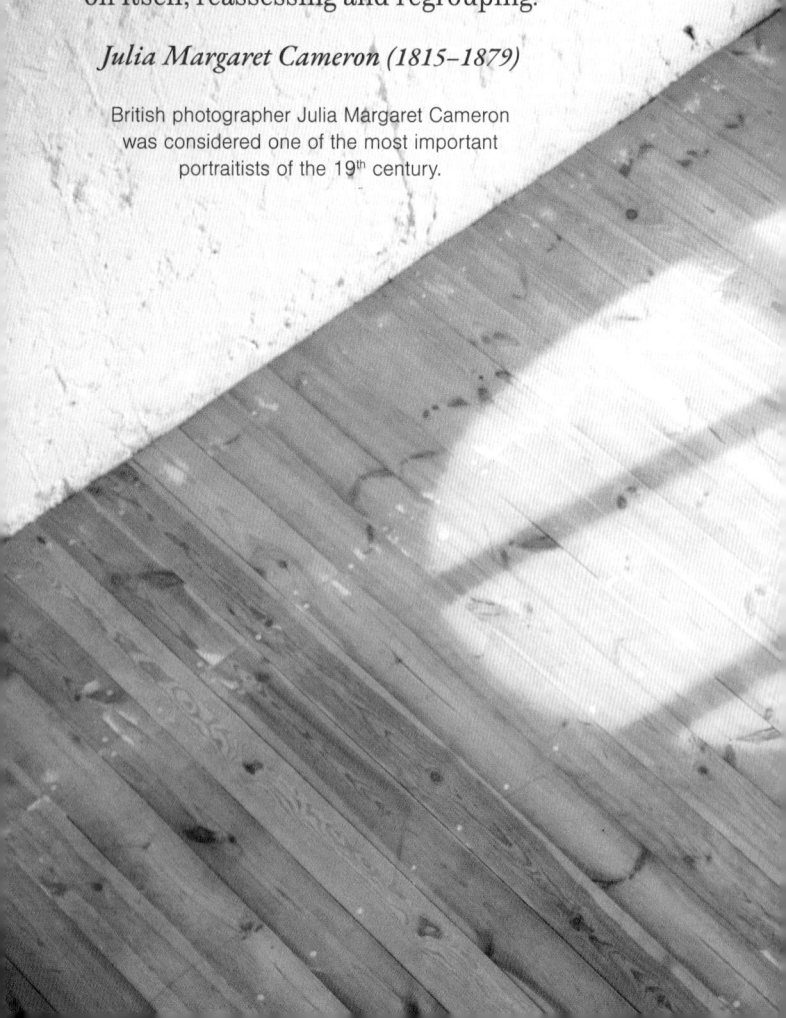

Your life, your choice...

make it a better one

*Every part of the journey
is of importance to the whole.*

Teresa of Ávila (1515–1582)

A prominent Spanish mystic, nun, and author of spiritual
classics, Teresa of Ávila was the originator of
the Carmelite Reform.

NOT WHAT WE EXPERIENCE, BUT HOW WE PERCEIVE
WHAT WE EXPERIENCE, DETERMINES OUR FATE.

Marie von Ebner-Eschenbach
(1830–1916)

Marie von Ebner-Eschenbach was an Austrian writer with keen observations and insights on life and society who portrayed life among both the poor and the aristocratic.

It's so nice to be a spoke in the
wheel, one that helps to turn,
not one that hinders.

Gertrude Bell (1868–1926)

Gertrude Bell was an English
writer, archeologist, political
officer, and intrepid explorer.

I've always had the feeling that nothing is impossible if one applies a certain amount of energy in the right direction. If you want to do it, you can do it.

Nellie Bly (1864–1922)

Nellie Bly was an American journalist whose undercover investigation of deplorable conditions at an insane asylum led to improvements in the treatment of the mentally ill.

Can anything be sadder than
work left unfinished?
Yes, work never begun.

Christina Rossetti
(1830–1894)

Christina Rossetti was an English poet
well-known for writing *Goblin Market
and Other Poems*, a collection which
established her as a significant
voice in Victorian poetry.

There are as many
sorts of women as
there are women.

Murasaki Shikibu (c. 973–c. 1014)

A Japanese poet regarded as a medieval
feminist, Murasaki Shikibu wrote *The Tale of
Genji,* considered one of the world's first novels.

Wherever women gather together, failure is impossible.

Susan B. Anthony (1820–1906)

Susan B. Anthony was an American social reformer, abolitionist, and activist who played a pivotal role in the women's suffrage movement. Her work helped pave the way for the 19th Amendment (1920) to the U.S. Constitution, giving women the right to vote.

Step out into the brand-new day

Let us not be discouraged by the magnitude of the task ahead. Together, we can bring about change.

Sarah Parker Remond (1826–1894)

A free-born African-American radical, Sarah Parker Remond was a suffragist and anti-slavery activist who toured the US, Britain, Ireland, and abroad. She became a physician later in life.

Self-reliance is the fine road to independence.

Mary Ann Shadd Cary (1823–1893)

Mary Ann Shadd Cary was an American-Canadian trailblazing abolitionist, suffragist, educator, and journalist, and the first Black female newspaper publisher in North America.

STEPPING IN TIME,

WE WALK TOGETHER

What you want to ignite in others must first burn inside yourself.

Charlotte Brontë (1816–1855)

Charlotte Brontë was an English novelist and the eldest of the three Brontë sisters, best known for *Jane Eyre*.

TRUTH IS POWERFUL AND IT PREVAILS.

Sojourner Truth (c. 1797–1883)

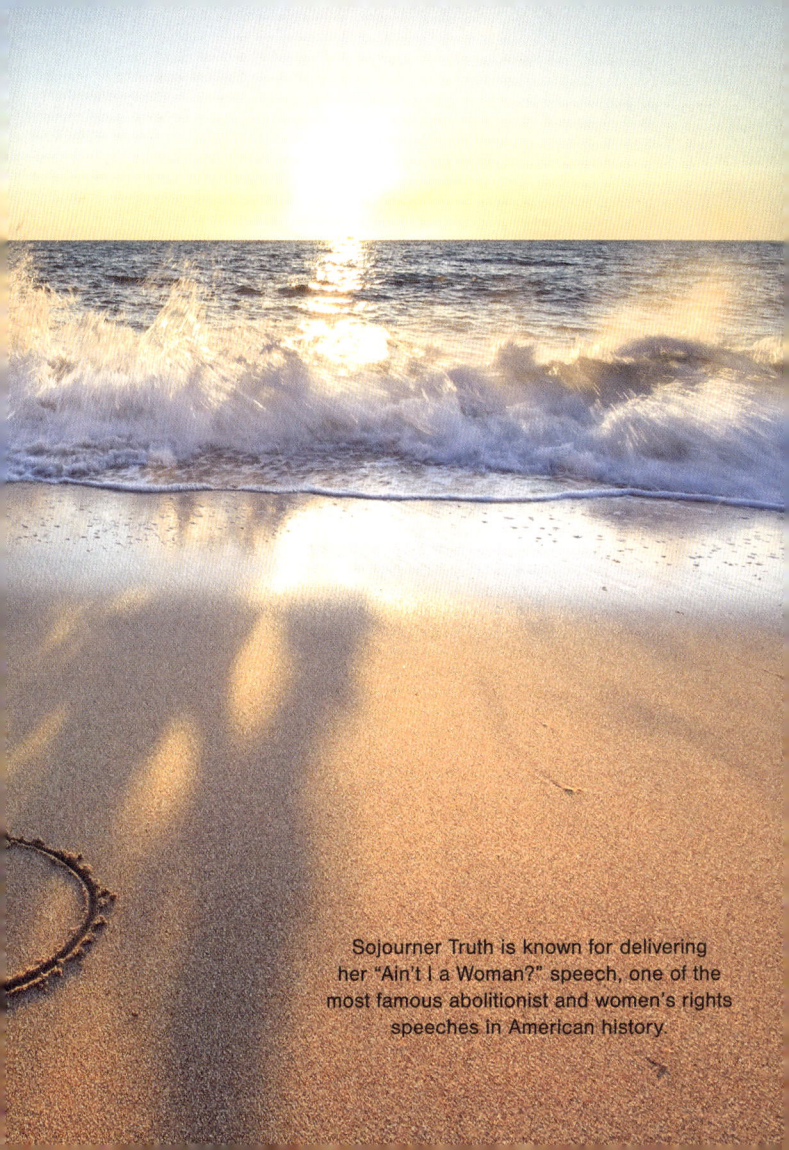

Sojourner Truth is known for delivering her "Ain't I a Woman?" speech, one of the most famous abolitionist and women's rights speeches in American history.

feel the
earth
beneath
your feet

THE STRONGEST PRINCIPLE OF GROWTH LIES IN THE HUMAN CHOICE.

George Eliot (1819–1880)

George Eliot was the pen name of Mary Ann Evans, English novelist, poet, journalist, translator, and one of the leading writers of the Victorian era.

Each small task of everyday life is part of the total harmony of the universe.

Thérèse of Lisieux (1873–1897)

French Carmelite nun Thérèse of Lisieux wrote the memoir *The Story of a Soul* (1898), which has become a modern spiritual classic.

DON'T EVER STOP. KEEP GOING.
IF YOU WANT A TASTE OF FREEDOM,
KEEP GOING.

Harriet Tubman (c. 1822–1913)

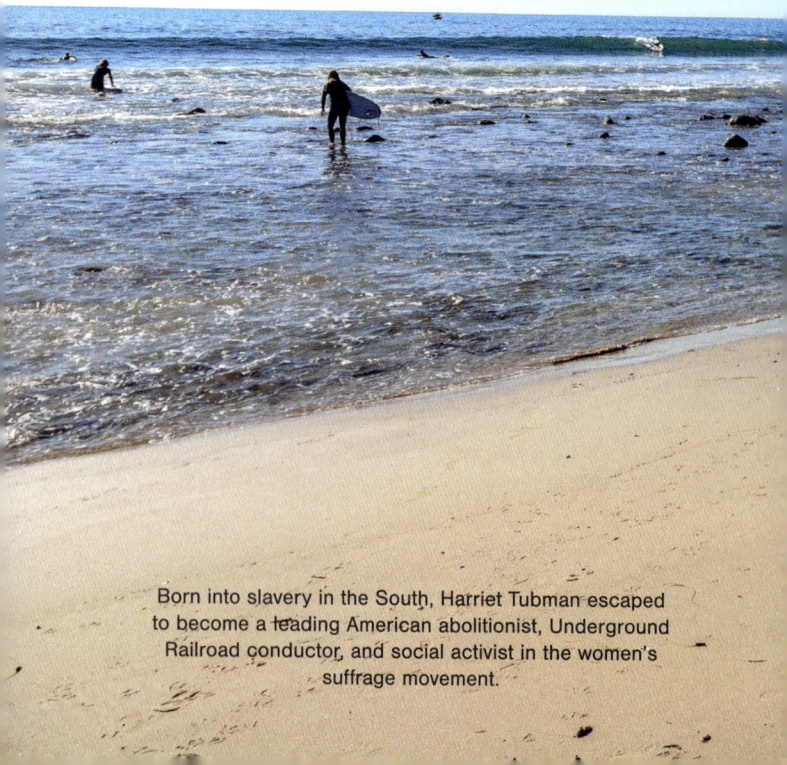

Born into slavery in the South, Harriet Tubman escaped to become a leading American abolitionist, Underground Railroad conductor, and social activist in the women's suffrage movement.

AS LONG AS I LIVE,
I WILL HAVE CONTROL
OVER MY BEING.

Artemisia Gentileschi (1593–c. 1656)

An Italian Baroque painter and the first woman to become a member of the Academy of Fine Arts in Florence, Artemisia Gentileschi depicted powerful and independent heroines, a revolutionary approach at the time.

I was annoyed from the start by the attitude of doubt by the spectators that I would never really make the flight. This attitude made me more determined than ever to succeed.

Harriet Quimby
(1875–1912)

American pioneering aviator, journalist, and film screenwriter Harriet Quimby was the first female to earn a pilot's license in the United States and to fly across the English Channel.

LUGLIO

BE A LIVING POEM

WE MAY MAKE
OUR FUTURE BY
THE BEST USE
OF THE PRESENT.
THERE IS NO
MOMENT LIKE
THE PRESENT.

Maria Edgeworth
(1768–1849)

Anglo-Irish novelist and educator
Maria Edgeworth challenged
societal norms and advocated for
positive change through her literary
works. She also made significant
contributions to the development
of the novel in Europe.

If we have had no past, it is well for us to look hopefully to the future—for the shadows bear the promise of a brighter coming day.

Frances Ellen Watkins Harper
(1825–1911)

Lecturer, abolitionist, suffragist, and author Frances Ellen Watkins Harper was one of the first African-American women to be published in the United States.

TRUTH IS STRONG, AND SOMETIME OR OTHER WILL PREVAIL.

Mary Astell (1666–1731)

Mary Astell was an English pro-feminist writer, who, as an advocate for equal educational opportunities for women, was considered to have radical views for her time.

I WANT TO DO EVERYTHING IN THE WORLD THAT CAN BE DONE.

Fanny Kemble (1809–1893)

English actress Fanny Kemble was also
a writer, social reformer, and abolitionist.

To aim at the best and to remain essentially ourselves is one and the same thing.

Janet Erskine Stuart
(1857–1914)

Janet Erskine Stuart was an English religious sister and charismatic leader who founded a number of schools and whose writings, both spiritual and instructional, reflect her lifelong quest for truth.

It is not easy to be a pioneer—but oh, it is fascinating!

Elizabeth Blackwell (1821–1910)

The first woman in the U.S. to earn a medical degree, and a life-long advocate for female doctors, Elizabeth Blackwell played an important role in both the United States and the United Kingdom as a social reformer.

Are you in?

I do not wish women to have power over men; but over themselves.

Mary Wollstonecraft (1759–1797)

Mary Wollstonecraft was a British writer, early advocate of women's rights to educational and social equality, and one of the founding feminist philosophers. She was the author of *A Vindication of the Rights of Woman*, a trailblazing treatise of feminism (1792).

I have just dropped into the very place I have been seeking, but in everything it exceeds all my dreams.

Isabella Bird (1831–1904)

The first woman to be elected as a fellow of the Royal Geographical Society, Isabella Bird was a pioneering English explorer, writer, photographer, and naturalist.

I have learned to live each day as it comes, and not to borrow trouble by dreading tomorrow.

Dorothea Dix (1802–1887)

Dorothea Dix was an American activist whose devotion to the welfare of the mentally ill led to widespread reforms in the United States and abroad. She recruited nurses during the Civil War and revolutionized modern nursing practices.

The keen spirit seizes the prompt occasion.

Hannah More (1745–1833)

English writer and abolitionist Hannah More was
a leading philanthropist and an active campaigner
for education for the poor.

If you have knowledge, let others light their candles at it.

Margaret Fuller (1810–1850)

American teacher and author Margaret Fuller wrote *Woman in the Nineteenth Century* which was considered the first major feminist work in the United States. She became one of America's first female foreign correspondents.

Although only breath, words which I command are immortal.

Sappho (c. 630–c. 570 BC)

A prolific Greek poet of antiquity, Sappho is known for her lyric poetry and innovation of first-person narration. Much of her poetry focuses on the lives and experiences of women.

Courage! Do not fall back.

Joan of Arc (c. 1412–1431)

Joan of Arc was a French visionary, early feminist, and symbol of freedom and independence, who as a military leader transcended gender roles and gained recognition as a savior of France.

MY SUN SETS TO RISE AGAIN.

Light tomorrow with today!

Elizabeth Barrett Browning (1806–1861)

An English poet of the Victorian era and a world-
famous writer in her day, Elizabeth Barrett Browning
made influential stands against social injustice.

Be

COURAGEOUS,

daring

AND

STRONG

I had only ordinary capacity but extraordinary persistency.

Maria Mitchell (1818–1889)

Maria Mitchell was the first female astronomer in the United States, first American scientist to discover a comet, and an early advocate for women in the sciences and pay equality.

Your destiny is always available

PHOTOGRAPHY CREDITS